SENIOR SC

"Thirteen Lives in Search of the Twelfth Grade"
Twelve Monologues and a Rap

By
JOHN-MICHAEL WILLIAMS

APPLAUSE
THEATRE BOOK PUBLISHERS
211 West 71 Street, New York, NY 10023

SENIOR SQUARE:
Thirteen Lives in Search of the Twelfth Grade

Copyright © 1987 Applause Theatre Book Publishers

LIBRARY OF CONGRESS CATALOGING -in-Publication Data

APPLAUSE THEATRE BOOK PUBLISHERS
211 W. 71st Street, New York, NY 10023
(212) 595-4735

for Tim Belden

Special thanks to Lavonne Mueller and Glenn Young,
and to the Spirit of Artesia High.

TABLE OF CONTENTS

Stage dark. *Senior Square* is an illusion, a place as alive in the imagination as it is in the real world. You may construct a simple, realistic set, or you may choose to suggest *Senior Square* with equally simple lighting and other effects.

ROCHELLE

A young girl carrying a large purse, combing her hair and looking into a hand mirror, walks on stage.

I'm goin' to a Madonna Film Festival at the public library tonight and, well — you never know *who* will be there, so it's always best to be beautiful.

(Sliding on a streak of lipstick)

Is that too much lipstick?

(Holding a small mirror up to her face and then looking up toward the sky)

This light is very bad — but a girl learns to cope. I'm gonna be an actress when I graduate. Then I'm changing my name from Mary Rochelle Ridgeway to Rochelle Ridge, though I hope the producers won't nickname me Rocky. Can you imagine? Rocky Ridge? *(Pause)* Though, on second thought — Rocky's kind of sexy don't you think? They call Raquel Welch "Rocky" and she's sexy, right? Yeah, Rocky Ridge. Does it sound too tough? *(Pause)* Well that's okay, because an actress has gotta be tough.

(Putting on eyeshadow)

9

Eyeshadow says it all, doesn't it? All the really famous actresses in America wear it. It's an American tradition — like apple pie, corsages on a date — hot dogs at a ball game — it's practically patriotic — just like Senior Square.

(Pointing)

That's it. Right in front of me.

(Horrified)

No, I can't step in! I'm only a sophomore and—

(Taking a small booklet out of her jacket and flipping it open)

— according to Chapter 3, Paragraph 6 of the Student Handbook, "Any non-senior apprehended within the boundaries of the Square is in violation of Article 6 of the Central High School Constitution regarding the essential traditions of the institution." I know. Heavy *stuff.* And if a senior catches you in there, you—

(Looking into the book again)

"Will be required to scrub the interior of Senior Square with a toothbrush or made to stand on your head during the Friday Pledge of Allegiance in the auditorium". I would just die.

(Dabbing on powder)

Seems like such a small thing, being able to walk inside a
brick enclosure and sit down, but for a lot of kids in my
school, Senior Square will never be anything more than
another broken dream. Many will not graduate for one
reason or another and you can never predict who'll make
it and who won't. Bobby Giangelo was voted most likely
to be elected Senior King, even though he was only a
sophomore and his twelfth grade days were two years
ahead of him. Bobby had it all, good looks, good grades,
good attitude, good family *(Pause)* good looks. *(Pause)* Oh
yeah, and money. Bobby loved school and everybody at
school loved him, but a lot of money can buy a lot of
cocaine and Bobby just burned out. Like a bulb that
glowed too bright for too long. "Socket warp" we call
it.

(Applying rouge)

Like the color? Oh, thank you. Rouge is very tricky. Too
little, you look anemic. Too much, you look like Ronald
McDonald. Other kids get bored, or married, or both,
then drop out. Some, just kinda fade away. And there are
the ones who get so close to Senior Square that they can
almost touch it but never make those last few steps. So, in
its own way, it's really somethin' special, something
everybody wants, though few kids will admit it. And
those who say that Senior Square is just a brick fence sur-
rounding a couple of picnic tables — those are the kids
who really want it the most. *(Pause)* I plan on having the
lead in the school play during my senior year. I truly
hope they'll do *Gone with the Wind.* Oh, I know it's a movie

but they can change it to a play for *me*. Scarlet O'Hara is a sweet frail, innocent young virgin in a desperate search for true love — a *perfect* role for me. *(Pause)* Don't you think so?

(She steps forth and becomes *Scarlet O'Hara)*

"I swear! As God is my witness — I will never be poor again!" Not bad, huh? And how about —

(Continuing performance)

"Prissy! Prissy! Quickly! Get me some rags and hot water. *(Pause)* Oh, hurry!"

(Looking in the mirror)

Hope I'm not too "pretty" for the part. Well, anyway — they can fix *that* with make-up. They can fix *anything* with make-up. Except Senior Square. This place needs more than a face lift! Look at the crab grass growing around that tree in the center of the square. You think so? Salt, to kill the weeds? Won't that hurt the tree too?

(Putting on eyebrow pencil)

Too much brow? No? Don't want to look like Brooke Shields. Oh, I know everybody says she's *so* pretty, but I think the biggest chunk of a girl's sex appeal is in her eyebrows and well, get a close up of Brooke's brows and you'd swear you're staring eye-to-eye with one of the

Muppets. *(Pause)* And if I won the role of Scarlet O'Hara, they'd *have* to cast Spike Paletti as Rhett Butler. He's the biggest hunk in the whole school; who *else* could they get for a part like that? Sure. Spike would get the lead. We'd date during the run of the play; that's very common between leading men and starlets. Then I'd have to break it off at the close of the performance because my career must *always* come first.

(Pretending to talk to Spike)

What? Yes, Spike, I *know* I'm the only woman you've ever loved, the only woman you ever *could* love *and* — the only woman you ever *will* love, but life must go on; our time has come and gone. The moment is over. *(Pause)* Yes, Spike, I *know* I've broken your heart and that I've ruined you forever for all other women. Uh, huh — I *am* aware that you'll never get over this, but Spike, darling, I told you from the beginning that *I* was an actress, so you really didn't dare to think that I'd choose a man over my career? You did? Oh Spike. Call me in Hollywood the next time you go to the coast. We'll have lunch. *(Pause)*

(Looking up and down, in all directions)

I like the way the Square looks right now — the orange light sinking into the cracks between the bricks and lighting up all the carved-in initials of seniors who left their mark over the years. My initials are gonna be inside there one day — in about a year and a half when I'm not a sophomore or a junior anymore. I'm gonna be one of the kids who makes it; don't ask me why, I just feel it.

(Pause)

And once I've graduated and won the Academy Award, I'd like to come back here and leave an impression of my hands and feet in a slab of wet cement, right in the center of Senior Square. The students would be so proud to have their own little slice of Hollywood Boulevard preserved forever in their school, and well, I wouldn't mind doing it all, even though it would be time snatched from my very busy and super-important schedule. I believe that a famous actress has to do things like that — even if she isn't paid. She's somehow got to thank all the loyal folks who each kicked in their six bucks at the box office. So I'd make the time to do this one small favor for my fans. The Square's a big part of the history of our school, you know. Senior boys who were graduating and then going into the service to fight in Vietnam partied in the Square the night before they went overseas. Private First Class Allan Des Moines, a former senior in this school —

(Pointing to the square)

— that's his initials right there; he won the Medal of Honor for bravery above and beyond the call of duty. That's right. He saved the lives of several Campus Corp officers when he ran into a barracks next to the gym and dragged out five senior soldiers who'd been knocked out by smoke fumes as their quarters burned. He's in the Senior Square Heroes Hall of Fame now. My cousin Florence even *dated* him and said he isn't stuck up at all for a hero.

(Primping her hair)

Of course, I'll have to lighten my hair during the production of my first film. All the best screen beauties bleach their do's. That's real class.

(Pause)

And we've had our share of celebrities from this school too. Uh huh. Walkin' right out of Senior Square and into the big, bright lights. *Marian Lutsky?* Oh yeah — she went here. No one ever dreamed that she'd start her own cookie franchise and become famous in *two* different states. And it all began in Mrs. Futzberger's Home Economics class — right here in our school. Marian, she added some coconut to Mrs. Futzberger's Raspberry Supreme cookies. And, well, the rest is history. There was no contest the year that Marian Lutsky entered the Senior Square Bake-off Competition. Georgette Samson had won the year before, but she was livin' in a dream world to think that her "Lemon Dainties" could hold up against Marian's "Coconut Raspberry Lutsky Bars." Heard Georgette's workin' in a drive-thru donut shop now. I remember when Marian's "Lutsky Bars" first arrived — just a week before she graduated? They were out of this world. I sent my grandma a box of 'em — all the way across the country. She's been tryin' to figure out the recipe for over a year, but she never seems to get it right. I heard that Marian's the *only* person alive who knows all the ingredients. Even the chefs in her bakeries aren't sure what's in that "magic pack" — the little pouch of goodies added to every batch? And I heard that "Lutsky Bars" are gonna be the *official* snack at the next world olympics. Yeah, Marian's really made a name for herself. *(Pause)* And then there was Paul Sterkly — what a man! He had the lead in the uptown Dinner Theatre's production of "The King and I." My mama took me to see it when I was still a kid — two years ago. Aunt Feena said he did a better job of it than Yul Brynner. The best part was, Paul came right off the stage and kissed me on the cheek just as the intermission lights came on. Almost dropped the meat loaf right off my plate. Imagine, the King of Siam kissing me in front of everyone at the classiest place in town. Oh, I'd love to study acting with him one day. Paul Sterkly — The King! Senior Square celebrities! We had Rhonda Cummings, she was a runner up for Vanna White's job on "The Wheel of Fortune," and there was Dukey Stalmeier — the first high school drop-out to walk backwards from Los Angeles, California to Eugene, Oregon. And of course, Lenora Walton — she's invented the upholstery that they use on the seats in the space shuttle.

Senior Square is our stepping stone to fame and fortune. And a special place in a lot of other ways, too. My daddy kissed my mama for the first time after giving her a white orchid corsage right over there,

(Pointing)

— near the North wall of the Square. Mama always said she fought him off, but I never believed it. And through the years, so many kids in their last months of high school have sat inside these walls and dreamed of where they'd go after graduation day. They planned their lives and struggled to say goodbye to the final days of being young.

(Pause)

Air's gettin' heavy out here this evenin', lotta humidity. And I want to get to that film festival before dark and before this dampness makes my hair friz up. I wish I could invite ya into Senior Square for a while, but I'd be wearin' out the bristles of my toothbrush tomorrow morning if I got caught.

(Feeling her hair)

Humidity's good for the plants I suppose —

(Looking in the mirror again and dabbing at her face)

But it's absolute *death* for your make-up, so I have *got* to split!

(Putting away cosmetics)

Well, have a nice evenin' and please don't go into Senior

Square after I'm gone. It's just one of those things that
really has to be earned. Just like the Academy Award.

(Fade out)

* * * * *

RAYMO

Hi. I'm Raymo, I'm a freshman, I'm cool, I'm happenin', I'm with it, I dig bein' a freshman and that's good, because I been one for three years. Yeah, I've taken English 1-A so many times, I can practically diagram a sentence under water. I *love* bein' a freshman, but I sure hope this is my last year in the ninth grade. My little brother was just goin' to Junior High when I started High School and next year *he'll* be a freshman and I would just completely freak out if my little brother and I was in the same class. So, I'm really tryin' hard this year. And it's not the books that give me the problem — it's *reading* the books that give me the problem. And those stupid classes! Now take Sex Education. Is that somethin' that you can learn in a classroom by watching movies of frogs? I remember back on my first day of Sex Education, I says to the teacher — Hey Miss Lopez, let's skip the class, I'm ready for the final exam! She was not a-mused, Miss Lopez. She was not a-mused last year either and this year, she is *severely* not a-mused. So that's S.E., right? Now, what about History? I mean, help me out, I just don't get it. Everybody did what they did, it's over with, so who needs to know about it? Right? So what if I *do* remember on what day World War One started? Am I gonna be able to stop somethin' that already happened by just remembering the day? Hey! It's over with! My mama always says "Don't cry over spilled milk." That's my attitude about History. It's spilled milk — so don't cry over it. And English *(Pause)* now there is a *heavy* waste of time. I mean, either you can talk or you can't. Right? I don't see the point in learning a bunch of words nobody can pronounce or spell anyway. It just don't make no sense. And Math? Forget about it. I got a calculator, Einstein's *already* discovered the theory of relativity, I ain't goin' to Europe so I don't need to know the Metric System —leave me alone! Ninth grade is drivin' me crazy! And how about that required foreign language? Lay a little mercy on me please. I mean, my father's a mechanic, his father was a mechanic, his father was a mechanic and his father was unemployed. What do you think the chances are that I'll be spending my summers in France? This English thing is foreign enough for me so let's get this out of the way before we boldly go where no ninth grader has gone before. And ya know what class *really* messes with my head? *Art!* That ain't no class for a *serious* dude to deal with. They say I should paint somethin'. You think I should paint somethin'?

(He pulls a can of spray paint out of his jacket and begins to enthusiastically shake it up and down)

Okay! I'll do a painting for ya! Right on the side of Senior Square! Whatchu like? My initials or the Iron Cross?

(Shaking the can again)

How 'bout my initials *on* the Iron Cross? *(Pause)* What? You're jokin' with me. How could *my* initials de-face school property? Uh-h-h-h-h.

(As he puts the can away)

Well, maybe you're right. I think a piece like this would
hang better on the side of the gym anyway. *(Pause)* My
cousin, Wedgie? Goes to a junior college outa state? He
tells me in *his* painting class they got a naked girl that sits
on a piano so you can sketch her. Now *that's* art! Know
what's sittin' on the piano in *my* art class? A wooden
doll.

A cheap, two foot high, wooden doll. And it ain't even
naked! Naw. Art ain't *no* class for a *serious* dude. So let's
get to P.E. Now there's a sensible class. I like P.E. — got a
B minus. It's a sensible class. You put on shorts, you go
outside, you run around, you throw the baseball, you do
a couplea pushups boom! — You get the B minus. What's
the problem? Know what you gotta do to get a B minus in
English? Man, you gotta read a play! No, I'm serious
here. You gotta read a *whole* play. You ever read a play? I
mean, we're talkin' Mission Impossible time, here. First,
you read the name of the person talking and just as
you're gettin' into what they're sayin' — boom! They go
an do somethin' and then you gotta look all the way to the
edge of the page to these giant letters and then wham! You
lose your place and you gotta look back up and read what
they're talkin' about again; it's a nightmare! Why can't
they just make school into a TV show? Yeah, like you sit
home twice a week and watch The English Show — about
a family that uses all these hard to pronounce words. You
see some action, you see some chicks, you hear some
tunes and then, durin' the commercial, you'd call in and

say, Hey! It's Raymo, I'm watchin' The English Show.
And the teacher says: "Yeah, what's it about tonight?"
Then you tell her, she gives you a B minus, you hang up
and turn on Miami Vice! *(Pause)* I'm just scared that I'll
be gettin' my first social security check before I get to
Senior Square.

I mean, what's a guy gotta do? I've almost done my four
years in high school, so I think they should make me an
honorary Senior Square member next year, even though
I'll only be a sophomore. *(Looking upward)* I *pray* I'll be a
sophomore. I could go in there anyway, if I really wanted
to, but I don't. *(Pause)* Uh, listen, I gotta split now. Okay?
Tomorrow, we're havin' a fitness test in P.E. and I wanna
get home and study.

* * * * *

SUZANNE

An "obviously pregnant" young girl walks on stage.

Next year I'll be sitting in Senior Square in a white dress, combing my hair and watching the bluebirds nest in the hollow ends of the goal posts. Nicky and I will be married by then, and I'll be a high school bride with a baby and a husband. Nicky's gonna marry me. Yes he is. Soon as he gets back to town. Oh, I know what you're all thinking. You're thinking Nicky isn't coming back. And you know — you could be right. I'm not dumb enough to think that I'm the first lady in the world who found herself in this situation. When the true love train leaves town, it's always the woman that gets left holding the baggage.

(She pats her stomach)

If Nicky doesn't come back, my life *will* continue. I believe that. And I'm *not* droppin' out of school either. That simply isn't an option. If it's necessary, my baby will be the first non-senior to officially get into Senior Square. 'Cause I'll take him there. Sure. Everybody 'ill talk. They'll point and whisper behind my back. But what can they really say? I mean, I'll come strolling into home room with a three ring binder under one hand and a baby anda pack of pampers 'neath the other. There's no excuse not to finish your education. It's easier for some and tougher for others, but you can get through — if it's really important to you. And it is, to me.

23

My sister Nadine dropped out when she got married. Said she'd finish up the following year. That was over ten years ago, and she's still a high school drop out. Not me. Suzanne Burns is going to graduate come hell or high water — twins or triplets. I'm not letting anybody or anything come between me and my future.

That ole Nicky. Fulla promises and bull. I fell for his chestnut eyes and his manly muscles. And I fell for 'em more than once.

(Emphatically)

Well — you haven't seen him! You might 'av taken a tumble yourself. Can't blame it all on him. Coulda said no.

(Patting her stomach)

But I didn't. I know it's silly, but I just somehow felt that a good girl couldn't get pregnant until she was married. Little more education on the birth control level woulda been more helpful to me than a high school diploma last year. Well. My Aunt Patty says "Life is a series of mistakes punctuated by death." Yep — she's a *real* inspiration. *(Pause)* I saw this stroller down at Taylor's Department Store? It had a two-seater up front, a little red awning on top, a place in the back for your books and a tiny TV tray on the side so you can watch your soap operas in between classes. Taylor's calls it "The Young Mother's Back to School Special," and I'm gonna get me one when the baby comes. I hope it's a boy.

If it is, I'm gonna name him Nicky — unless Nicky doesn't come back to marry me in which case I'll name him Sidney. Sidney's the guy I used to go out with and Nicky *hates* him. *(Pause)* Gotta get your justice wherever you can. If I have a girl, I'll probably name her Tina, after Tina Turner. Or maybe, Madonna, after Madonna. How 'bout Tina Madonna Burns? You like it? Thanks. 'Course, if Nicky marries me, that'll be out because his last name is Sarfonna. Can you imagine? Tina Madonna Sarfonna?

By the time I get out of high school, my baby will be one year old. When I get my college degree — prob'ly in General Education — he'll be five and starting kindergarten. See, I was a girl who thought I knew everything, but —

(Patting her stomach)

— not quite. I'll prob'ly get a Masters in Psychology, so that I can figure *myself* out. And maybe I can help some other young girls get to Senior Square *before* they get pregnant. Then, I'll prob'ly wrap it all up with a Doctorate in Sociology. *Dr.* Suzanne. I like it! Why not? Start my own clinic for young women. We need stuff like that. Wish I could have had a place to go where I could'av talked to someone before I made the decision to be a guest in the back seat of Nicky's car.

(Touching her stomach)

Oops! — I felt him move. *(Laughs)* Or *her* move. Or *them* move. I could have that fancy test to find out if there's more than one, but I want to be surprised. Like opening a box of Cracker Jack. Besides — that test is expensive! I'd rather spend the money on a new pair of Reboks. I'm not rich like Wookie Pennsicola. 'Course he earns all his extra cash beating people up for money. Lord — what if it was triplets? Hmmmm. That would sure do it for the breast feeding idea.

(Pointing to center stage)

Where'd that come from? Right over there. Sometimes I wish I were a flower. Just like that daisy — the yellow one growing right next to that tree in the center of Senior Square. Life seems so much easier for them. Except for that one maybe. Ground is hard here — 'course, on the other hand, it didn't have to take Trig with Mr. Dromaderry — . Wonder if it had as hard of a time gettin' to Senior Square as I'm havin'? *(Pause)* I'll bet one of the senior boys, like Spike Paletti, will yank it up as soon as they see it. But for right now anyway — it's doin' okay and most flowers have it made. — No tryouts for cheerleading and no stupid first kisses. All they have to do is stand there and wait for a bee to come along and get 'em pregnant. And they don't expect the bee to stick around afterwards, so they never feel jilted or bummed out. Flowers do okay. 'Course they can never go to the movies or order out for pizza, but ya can't have it all.

Senior Square. I'll make it. No problem. Nicky always

says that you can't become a victim of the future — you got to take hold of it and create your own opportunities.

(Pause)

Well,

(Patting her stomach)

that boy's done enough "creating" for now. Listen, I gotta split! Lots 'a homework to do 'n stuff *and* ya never know who might call. But if that phone don't ring — I won't be alone. I've still got my baby. And I've still got me.

(Pause. Then looking toward the center of the square.)

Spike Paletti, if you pick that flower, I'm gonna hire Wookie Pennsicola to turn your *head* into a flower arrangement!

(Fade out)

* * * * *

PAT

This monologue begins offstage with Pat shouting as she delivers her flyers.

PAT. *(Voice over)*
Ban high school, now! Stop the oppression of the teenage masses by the practice of forced education!

(She walks onto the stage carrying a stack of flyers)

Pat Johnson for Senior Square President! Ban high school now! Stop the oppression of —

(Offering the audience a flyer)

Here. Take one. Don't you wanna learn about the oppression of the teenage masses? 'Sposed to be a free country — but just try to drop out of high school before you're eighteen and see what happens. Think about it. Forced education. It's like slavery or prison. Locking you up inside a dirty yellow room — fillin' your mind with History, Math, Social Studies — all *kinds* of propaganda. *(Pause)* Yeah.

They burn the eyes out of rabbits with chemicals in order to test mascara. Think about it. God *knows* what horrors they commit when whippin' up a batch 'a lipstick. And ya know, hair spray destroys the ozone layer in the atmosphere — that thin wrapper of clear gas that protects us from ultraviolet rays? The little buggers that cause skin cancer? Oh sure. You'll all have beautiful hair-dos — but no skin! Think about it. And then, if they have just one teeny, tiny leak from a nuclear power plant, your hair falls out anyway so what's the point? Thank you.

(Shouting)

Senior Square is a sexist structure built by oppressive men who want to control the culture through the use of teenmalienation — Yeah. Teen-may-lee-in-ation — the brutalization of teenagers by forcing them to go to school. And let me tell ya somethin.'

(She takes a piece of paper out of her jacket)

Here's some interesting factual data on the history of Senior Square. Charles McPhillips, Senior Square President, 1984. Walden Ash, Senior Square President, 1985. Christifa Sambor, Senior Square President, 1986. Timothy Belden, Senior Square President, 1987. Now, what do *all* of the former presidents of Senior Square have in common? I'll give ya a little hint — none of them will ever have a baby! Pat Johnson is going to be the first woman president of Senior Square! Think about it. Me, Pat Johnson, in control of a sexist structure built by oppressive men! Yeah. And Pat's a great name, too, because when you write somebody a letter, they don't know if you're a man or a woman — makes 'em crazy. I like that. Wait til I'm the president of Senior Square. I'll radicalize this place — bring the struggle of the *people* into these walls. Redecorate. Rip out these old, faded, beaten, bashed-in bricks of yesterday and replace 'em with the shiny new, high tech slabs of liberation. A political overall — designed by The Revolution Renovation Service.

I mean, you can't take all that stuff your parents dish out. Does your mother tell you how to dress? Yeah — I thought so. When your mother tells you not to wear jeans, you're bound by an allegiance to all the kids of the world to live in denim for at least the next seven days. Do they ever give you advice on dating? *(Pause)* Uh huh. They want you to go out with the *right* kind of people. You know — dogs? That's when you gotta find yourself somebody slick and stupid. Preferably a creature whose hair is at least *three* different colors. Bring 'em home and let your parents get the impression that you just might *marry* this person. And the more they criticize them, the *more* you talk about the wedding. Then when they absolutely forbid you to ever see that person again — that's when you set the wedding date. Think about it. Parents give advice out of guilt. They don't really expect you to follow that stuff.

See, parents are in the business of making impressions. They wanna make impressions on their bosses, on the neighbors, on the checkout people at the store. They're on stage for "The Joneses," know what I mean?

They've given up on exploring the purpose of their existence. The most mysterious, unanswered question in my parents' lives is: *"What are we going to do about Pat?"* Becoming an adult can sure take you out of the fast lane and put you on a slow journey to nowhere. Grow up and you lose your ability to change — to learn. No point in telling my parents about the sad state of the world — can't hear if ya don't listen. Yeah. And I've tried to raise the consciousness of other students too — but you know what they say to me? They say, "Hey Pat — I don't wanna get involved!"

(Shouting)

News Bulletin! News Bulletin! News Bulletin! If you were *born* — you're involved! Life *is* a demonstration. Make a sign. Fight the fight. Boldly go where no woman has gone before —

(Loudly)

— to the Presidential Podium of Senior Square! The place where you begin to change the world is right here.

Cancer, Aids, Sexism, Nuclear War, Teenage Suicide, Drug Addiction, Environmental Pollution and Dead Rabbit Eyeliner. And here's the *real* nightmare — in only twenty years these will be the good old days! *Think about it.*

(She exits, shouting)

Ban high school now! Stop the spraying of hair! Save a rabbit — drop the mascara habit! Pat Johnson for President!

(Fade out)

* * * * *

THE RAPPER

A high-style, young black man carrying a **huge** *ghetto blaster radio, struts out to center stage and does a hip rap about Senior Square. He begins by talking as the rap beat thumps in the background. It's a drum, synthesizer instrumental. A break dance, or parts of one, may be performed in conjunction with the rap, if desired.*

Doin' time. Time. Time. Doin' time.
Doin' time. Time. Time. Doin' time.
Senior Square? Yeah, I see.
Once you're there — man you're free!

Some say school's a learnin' fac-to-ry,
To me, it's just a peni-tenti-ary.
Doin' time. Time. Time. Doin' time.
Doin' time. Time. Time. Doin' time.

They lay it on your body,
Lay it on your soul,
You're locked up till the summer,
Then you're on parole.
And when the summer's over,
Dude you're back in jail,
So ya better bite the bullet,
And try hard not to fail.
Doin' time.

Yeah. I'm talkin' 'bout —
Doin' time. Time. Time. Doin' time.
P.E., S.E., G.E.D.. Biology, History, L, M, N, O, P.
Learnin', burnin', study hard,
The gates of school are like a prison yard.
Class room. Cell block. 's all the same,
They should give you a number, 'cause they *never* learn
your name.
Mama. Dad-dy. Who are you?
Don't know who you are,
An' don't know what to do.
Make a break for freedom,
If you dare to strive,
But the dogs just track you down,
Bring ya back alive.
To the school yard gate,
In you come,
And you find that you are back,
Where you had star-ted from.
Run man if you want to,
But you cannot run too far,
School is just a prison and you *Are:*
Doin' time. Time. Time. Doin' time.
Doin' time. Time. Time. Doin' time.

(Shouting)

Yo!

"Yo" is a hip way of saying "hello".

(Louder)

I said. YO!
How do you spell that anyway?

(Looking offstage. Shouting)

Nathan!

(Louder)

Yo, Nathan!

(Then he just shrugs)

Snuck my favorite girlfriend,
Right into the gym,
Got her by the football coach,
Slipped 'er right past him.
Kissed her near the locker room,
Man she made me proud,
Then the teachers kicked her out,
No vis-itors allowed!
Doin' time. Time. Time. Doin' time.
Doin' time. Time. Time. Doin' time.

Senior Square. Sen-ior Square.
Gate to free-dom —

(Pointing at the Square)

It's right there.
So close to me,
But far a-way,
No re-prieve for you,
Till grad-u-ation day.
Don't stand a chance for — a special fav-or,
No time off for *good* be-havior.

Monday through Friday,
Nine to three,
How can the Board of Ed,
Lay this rap on me?
I got girls to date,
Games to play,
A social life to lead,
And school gets in the way.
The weekend comes,
And you get down,
But be-fore you know it —
Monday morning comes around.
I could use a break,
Wouldn't mind a little slack,
But skip a couple days 'a school,
They jump right on your back.

Sister, brother help me out,
Learnin' drives me nuts and makes me wanna shout:
Doin' time. Time. Time. Doin' time.
Doin' time. Time. Time. Doin' time.

(Kids screaming to the tune of the song "Chain Gang.")

That's the sound of the kids,
Workin' on their fi-nals.
Yeah that's the sound of the kids,
Workin' on their fi-i-nals.

Yeah, they lay it on your body,
Lay it on your soul,
You're locked up till the summer,
Then you're on parole.
And when the summer's over,
Dude you're back in jail,
So ya better bite the bullet,
And try hard not to fail.
Do that time.
Hang in.
Stand in.
Your four, too.
And they will
Have to give,
That freedom back to you.
You may not wanna run right into Senior Square,
But it's easier than droppin' out,
And better than the chair!

Doin' time. Time. Time. Doin' time.
Doin' time. Time. Time. Doin' time.

Senior Square? Yeah, I see.
Once you're there — man you're free!

(Talking to audience, as he walks off)

And I ain't doin' no more than four! Know what I'm talkin' 'bout? Diploma — then *homa!* I'm outa here.

(As he exits)

I'm history, man. *I am gone.*

(Fade out)

*****

NATHAN

Enter Nathan, horned-rimmed glasses, clumsy. Awkward, strange looking.

Next semester, I'll be the only junior to ever sit in Senior Square. They're passing me from junior to senior in the same year. I'm a 4.0 kinda guy. Straight A's my whole life — even in kindergarten. Makes the other kids hate your guts. They'll probably beat me up next term when I eat lunch in the square for the first time, but I am accustomed to the uncouth animalistic behavior of the lower classes. Intelligence has always bred contempt.

(Pause)

Academics are no problem for me whatsoever. I appear to be equally brilliant in all subjects, breezing through Trigonometry to Latin and on to the three different foreign languages that I speak fluently. French? Ma oui! German? Ya vol! Texan? Y'all come! I have a photographic memory, have memorized *forty-seven* pages of the O.E.D.—

(Taking a large dictionary out from his back pocket)

The O.E.D.? Oh, sorry — The Oxford English Dictionary. Yeah, and one day, I'm sure I'll have the entire thing entered into

(Tapping his forehead)

the ole frontal lobes. I've memorized the definition and spelling of every word from Aardvark (an African mammal of the order of Edentata and the genus Orycteropus) to Aphid (a small homopterous insect of the family Aphididae). Aardvark to Aphid may not sound like much to you, but if you take the time to check, you'll see 627 entries within those boundaries. And I know the spelling and meaning of *everyone* of 'em! Ya don't think so, uh?

(Holding out an imaginary piece of paper)

Well, here's the list. Come on. Give me one!

(Pause)

Huh? Okay. Accrementition? Aw come on — I thought you'd pick a hard one! Okay. Accrementition.

(He spells it out)

A-c-c-r-e-m-e-n-t-i-t-i-o-n. Accrementition. Growth by the addition of similar cells. Like juvenile hall is an accrementition to Folsom Prison. You know? The "similar cells" thing? Got another one?

(Pause)

Animadvert? Yike, is this like nursery school or somethin'? Okay. Animadvert.

(He spells it out)

A-n-i-m-a-d-v-e-r-t. Animadvert. To consider or remark by way of criticism, or censure. To express censure. Like Mrs. Turdles animadverted my sociology paper on "Sexuality and the Liberated Teen." Hit me again! Antinomy?

(Pause)

Frontwards or backwards? Yeah, just kidding. Antinomy.

(He spells it out)

A-n-t-i-n-o-m-y. Antinomy. Opposition of one law or rule to another law or rule. Like the school dress code is an antinomy to fashion. Yeah, and by the way — there are *two* types of Aardvarks in the various regions of Africa. Math? Well, I can add, subtract, multiply and divide even the most complex mathematical problems without the use of a calculator. Who groaned? Doubt is a disease of the faithless! Give me a mathematical problem.

25 times 73? Please don't insult me — I'm a very intelligent person. I want a *real* mathematical problem. Okay! 9 times 6 plus 16 minus 6 divided by 4 plus 113. Ah! The inevitable and familiar 129! Next! 3 plus 3 plus 3 times 542 minus 63 plus 2.5? You mean the ole 508.5? — One of my favorites.

Ya, I'm smart but I am *not* a happy person, for I live in the wake of unfulfilled fantasy because, my dream is to be the star of the football team — a desire that is quite unlikely to be addressed since I am one of the most physically uncoordinated human beings to ever inhabit the planet terra firma. I mean, I fall down when I'm walking across a room never mind trying to carry a football over a field while wearing spike shoes and a twelve-pound steel helmet. But I still wanna be a football player. No — I would *not* be satisfied with being on the *Soccer* team. Soccer is *not* a sport for intelligent people. No game that requires you to hit *anything* with your head is a game for intelligent people — unless of course you're wearing a helmet.

(Pause)

Thank you very much, but I believe that Croquet is an activity for those of us who are approaching our late eighties. And don't bother to suggest baseball. That stick separates you from any real challenge. No, football is the *only* real sport. It's *you* against *them*. Your body against theirs. No bats, no mitts. Just bone against bone. A true, civilized sport. But alas, I'm a genius, not a football hero.

In the boy scouts, I memorized the entire manual on the first day, Chapter 19, Paragraph 2, Care of your camping equipment during adverse weather conditions? Fascinating! But then I fell over my own lap and landed on my head while trying to tie my shoelace. It's klutz city and for

all of my intellectual prowess and frankly, brilliance, I
have been, for a lifetime, deprived of the glories of physi-
cal coordination, a situation that has left me both frus-
trated and defeated. I dream of leaping over Senior
Square on a windy day and catching the final pass thrown
way out of the football field and over the goal posts. I
long to roll on the cool cement of the square, scratching
and bruising my face as I taste the victory of winning the
inner city high school playoff championship for the ole
alma mater. I *lust* after the dream of being carried by my
team mates through the crowds of screaming fans and
groping cheerleaders, all yelling out Nathan! Nathan!
Nathan! — with the enthusiasm of a nation bidding
welcome to its number one war hero.

I covet the taste of the homecoming queen's lips on my
thin, underdeveloped mouth as the sweat pours off my
forehead and my eyes are blinded by the endless stream
of flashbulbs capturing one picture after another, each
amateur photographer hoping for the shot of me that will
be chosen for the cover of the high school annual. I
wanna be popular! I mean, just to have a girlfriend,
someone who could get over my un-Bruce Spring-
steenish appearance and fall madly in love with my
brain. A female who could get hot for my cerebellum. I
had a girl once — in the sixth grade. Eloise Turtzly. — A
nice girl. But she eventually dropped me because she
couldn't take the harassment from the other kids. She
told me I was a sweet guy but said I reminded her too
much of the various insects that they show close-ups of
on those TV nature shows.

I wanna be liked! But alas. I fear that next semester I will be just another brilliant wimp sitting in Senior Square pathetically consuming a soggy tuna fish sandwich and watching all the lucky brain-dead jocks kiss the girls and sop up an athlete's glory. Such hopeless plunderings are dreams — always taking us farther than reality can ever go. But, I suppose that Albert Einstein never made it to the cover of *Sports Illustrated* either.

(Pause)

Well, I should be getting home now.

(Holding up his finger)

I sense the barometric pressure to be going higher and higher and I predict a large formation of cumulus clouds in the very immediate future. — It's gonna get cold.

(Walking away and softly cheering)

Nathan! Nathan! Nathan! Nath—

(Fade out)

*****

JACK

A jock shuffles out onto center stage. He's bouncing a basketball as he enters.

Hey Senior Square!

(Looking around)

I'm almost a senior so I guess you wouldn't mind if I just slip in and get a feel for bein' in the center of the universe.

(He moves back toward the square and then looks up)

Uh-h-h-h

(Shouting)

No Coach! No, I wasn't goin' into Senior Square. Not me. Just gettin' a closer look at a couple of initials. Thought I saw Sylvester Stallone's name on the — yeah coach. Yeah, I need my toothbrush to clean my teeth. Right. That's right. I need that brush so I won't be goin' into Senior Square. No sir. Last thing on my mind. Yeah, I'll be inside the auditorium in a couple of minutes. Just wanna work on my speech a little.

(Takes a piece of paper out of his jacket)

Take care coach.

(To audience)

Man's a monster. Gave me five laps this afternoon just for hitting Raleigh Treesland on the head. Five Laps! For no reason! Hey! I'm Jack. Jack Top 'o the World O'Riley. That's my nickname, 'cause I'm—

(Bouncing the ball three times)

— on top 'o the world, you know?

(Pause)

Yeah, another basketball season, another trophy. They-'re really starting to pile up on me. And the speeches are getting tougher and tougher to come up with. Let's see here, better rehearse this.

(Opens up paper and then puts it away)

Why do *I* always have to give some jive speech? They want me to talk about what I do on the basketball court? If I could really tell 'em what I have to say about basket-ball — I'd say — ladies and gentlemen:

(He rapidly bounces the ball up and down in a rhythmic movement, mimicing a conversation)

Yeah. Then I'd say, and furthermore:

(He bounces the ball in another emphatic pattern, as if in a speech)

And in conclusion, I'd like to add:

(He finishes up with a rapid, slam-bam routine, ending with a BOOM! BOOM! BOOM! of the basketball)

Thank you for listening.

(He tosses the ball offstage)

Ya know, I have been the captain of every team I've ever been on in my life since kindergarten. Football, baseball, volley ball, soccer — everything. I've been dating cheerleaders since the fifth grade, and havin' the *same* conversation with 'em. Oh, different cheerleaders, but the *same* conversation. It's hard to get close to a girl whose existence is focused around her pompoms. But they sure look good hangin' on your arm at the corner drive-in. I'm a high glory guy, what can I say? But you know what I *really* want more than anything else? I wanna get an A. No, I'm serious here. And I don't even care what subject it's in so long as it ain't sports. I mean, at this point, I'd take an A in Elementary Reading *anything* — one lousy A, that's all I want.

I'd like my ole man to open my report card one time without saying "Molly, who's the father of this idiot son of yours?" One time. The girls are nice, the trophies are nice, but I got to think about the future and what's that

gonna be for a grade B ball player with a D plus average?
Tough guy. That's me.

(Pause)

Betchu you never thought I used to run from fire as a
kid? — Hit the back door everytime my mama turned on
the stove; just scared 'a flames I guess. 'Fraid of alotta
things — dogs, older kids, girls, math class, the
mailman.

(Pause)

I used to be afraid of needles, too. When mama took me
to the doctor — she always made me promise not to cry.
But I was so afraid that I wet my pants while tryin'
not to cry.

(Pause)

Things in my life look good from the outside. Other guys
envy me. They think I got it wrapped up. Truth is, I'm
just barely makin' it. I'm tired, man. Tired to the bone —
tired to the core 'a the bone. But I made some
progress!

(He takes a syringe out of his coat and rolls up his sleeve)

I don't cry anymore.

(He ties a tourniquet around his arm)

And I sure got this needle thing whipped!

(He pulls out a small bag of heroin and pours the powder into a spoon)

Don't wet my pants anymore. Mosta the time.

(Lights a match and holds it under the spoon)

Hey! I don't run from fire anymore.

(A nervous laugh)

Cheerleaders just say Rah! Rah! Rah! Rah! Rah! That's a whole sentence to them.

(Sucking the dope up into the needle and then shouting)

Start without me tonight, coach!

(Another nervous laugh)

I'm gonna be a little late this evenin'.

(Pause)

Yeah, used to be scared 'a needles—

(Aiming the needle at his arm and pushing it in)

(Loudly) —but I'm not scared of 'em anymore.

(Pause)

'Cause I'm on top.

(Shouting)

I'm on top of the world!

(He collapses onto his knees with the needle still in his arm)

(Lights out)

*****

ARBADELLA

ARBADELLA is a hip black girl. She walks out with "an attitude" and stands firmly at Center Stage.

I'm Arbadella Washington, I'm fourteen years old, I'm black, I'm mean, I'm in the ninth grade and I'm goin' into the Senior Square. Oh? You don't think I will? Well, I'm gonna tell you somethin'. Miss Lola Johnson — the history teacher? The *evil* history teacher? I'm talkin' 'bout Frankenstein don't be chewin' gum if he came into that class, that Miss Johnson is so evil. Well, last semester, I stood right up in that history class, in front of everybody in the whole room and I says, real loud like, Miss Johnson, you is about the ugliest woman I ever saw in this town. No, no, I'm sorry Miss Johnson, you *is* the ugliest woman I ever seen, period. And that Miss Johnson told me to go to the principal and I sat right down at my desk and I says — if the principal wants *me,* he knows where I am. And she dismissed the class ten minutes early and rushed out of the room. That's right. *(pause)* An' I'm goin tell you somethin' *else* too. Last Spring, I went over to South Street Jack's Saloon, walked in the door, looked that ole bartender in the face and ordered myself a glass 'a hard whiskey. That man looked down at me and says "You got an ID?" And I says, yeah. *(making a fist)* This is my ID! And then he laughed and says "How old are you?"

And I said thirteen and a half. And he laughed again and
then gave me the whiskey. Uh-huh. And if I would go in
that bar, I would go in that square. And I will — in a
minute.

'Cause I am not in the mood to go up in there right now,
an' Arbadella Washington don't do nothin' when she
ain't in the mood and you can ask Richard Sheridan
'bout that. Richard tried to get "fancy" with me at the
movies last weekend. First he tried the ole "sneakin' the
arm roun' the shoulder durin' the scary part," and I
wopped him upside th' head with a box 'a Milk Duds but
it didn't knock no sense into him, 'cause on the way
home, he pulled his daddy's car over to th' side 'a th' road
an' tried to pull the "outa gas" on me. And I says,
Richard Sheridan — you come near me again, I mean
you even *think* of comin' near me and I will turn your
daddy's Se-dan into a convertible by puttin' your head
through the roof. So then, he tried to do "the beggar"
and says, "Arbadella, when you gonna lay some lovin' on
me honey babe?" And I says, when I am in the mood.
And he says, "When will that be?" And I says, when I'm
twenty-two years old and we've been married at least one
day. Then Richard, he commences to goin' crazy, talkin'
'bout how much *pain* he was in from bein' "love hungry"
and how he's in agony from lack 'a th' "fancy stuff" and I
just got right outa the car in the middle 'a nowhere,
'cause I *am* a lady an' I ain't listenin' to that kinda filth
from no pimply faced boy that don't even have his own
automobile. Got out and walked home, nearly a quarter
of a mile. That's right. So, if Richard Sheridan didn't

make me do "the honeymooner" with him, I sure ain't gonna let no senior-freak-jock get me to scrubbin' no cement patio with a toothbrush.

That's right. I am goin' into Senior Square. Right now. 'Cause it's almost dark, it's 'bout ta rain, an' ain't nobody gonna see me goin' in there anyway. All right! *(scraping her feet on the ground)* Don't wanna get that ole Senior Square dirty — here I go. *(stopping in a shocked look and shouting)* Miss Johnson! You look purty, in that dress this evenin'! *(pause)* No ma'am, I wasn't goin' into Senior Square ma'am, hunt-uh. I'm only a freshman — I'm *years* away from Senior Square. Yes Miss Johnson, it is gettin' late — I do think I'll be on my way home. You have a nice evenin' now. *(Making sure Miss Johnson is gone and then looking toward audience)* I'm comin' back. That's right. I'm walkin' 'roun the block, then comin' back and I'm goin' into Senior Square. *(as she walks off stage)* I'm goin' into that Senior Square. That ole hen don't scare me — I'm goin' in there and when I *get* in there, I'm gonna spit all over the place. That's right! *(fading out) I'm goin' into that square. I'm goin' in there to —*

(Fading out)

* * * * *

NUMBER 12

A nervous, "freaky" looking boy walks slowly to Center Stage and then stands still at the entrance to Senior Square.

Since I moved to America my life has really changed. Things are *very* different here. The culture is different, the language is different, the people are definitely different. It's hard to get used to — difficult to fit in, but I keep trying because I don't want everybody to just think of me as a "foreigner". I get real uptight when kids ask me about my home. I know they'd get upset if I told them about it, so I just change the subject.

Senior Square is the strangest thing I've ever seen and I've really been around. It's hard for me to understand why it's so important to everybody around here, although since I've been at Central High, I've started to find myself kind of attracted to it, too. I've got two years ahead of me before I'll be a senior, but when I finally walk into these walls, believe me — it's going to be a first. You see, I'm an illegal alien. Can you guess where I'm from? *(pause)* Mexico? No, sorry. Europe? *(pause)* No — but closer. Russia? Nope. Much farther than that. See, I'm from outer space. Yeah, I'm from another planet, so don't try to confuse me with facts about Senior Square. I'm a Kratonian — from the planet Kratonia? Guess you've never heard of it — it's in another solar system and believe me — I *don't* go home for Christmas vacation. Yep. My name is Number 12, but you can call me Joe.

My parents? Naw — we don't have parents on Kratonia;
we got test tubes. No, no we don't even got test tubes. No,
no. We come from pods. Yeah, yeah, that's it. Pods. We
grow out of pods — long, thin, shiny, *slimy* pods just like
the ones in "The Invasion of the Body Snatchers." No
one on Kratonia's figured out where the pods come from
yet — but they're lookin' into it.

No, don't remember much about the trip to Earth. I was
in a state of suspended — uh, suspended ani — *(pause)*
ani — *(pause)* I was *doped* out of my mind on some kinda
astro gas. Yeah, that's it, astro gas. Naw, naw. Ya can't get
it here. *(pause)* Huh? No, I don't have any left. Yes, I'm
sure, okay? Leave me alone. Don't bother me, ya know.
I'm from outer space and I could go crazy at any moment
if I'm bothered. And I *wouldn't* be responsible for what I
might do because I'm *not* an earthling so regular laws
don't apply to me.

Senior Square, huh? Yeah, I remember when I was a kid
back in Cleveland — I mean *Kratonia,* we had a place like
Senior Square — down near the corner gas station, I
mean, the rocket fuel base. We called it "The playground." Yeah, and ya had to live on our street to go into
the playground or else we'd *kick your* — I mean, we'd dis-
solve your face with a laser transport beam. And that can
be *real* messy.

School's tough, ya know? I got yelled at for fallin' asleep
in Math class last week? I tried to explain to Miss Dipper
that I have a problem stayin' awake because us folks from

Kratonia got two brains, ya know, and all that double thinkin' can make ya real tired. Then Miss Dipper says "If you have *two* brains — why did you get a "D" on your Algebra test?" And then she made me stand outside in the hall after I tried to explain how we operate under a different mathematical system in outer space.

I think I'll walk into Senior Square. Yeah, I know I ain't a senior yet, but I've been everywhere in the galaxy so I might as well wrap it all up with a stroll into the big brick box.

(Holding firmly onto his temples)

Yes — I recognize the thought patterns. It's the *entire* Varsity Football team. — They're sending me a message. Just a second, let me translate it from English into Kratonia. Uh, Ograk, do-wop *(pause)* A-diddy. Wop, wop. Rama lama, lama, lama, ding. Dong. Okay! I got it. They're sayin' "Joe, if you go into Senior Square, we are going to return you to your home in outer space by sending your *head* into orbit". Hm-mmmmmmmmmm. That's kinda discouraging. I mean, the thought of my head taking off on its own like that.

But I'll tell ya — Senior Square is *very* tempting to me right now. 'Cause you see, on Kratonia, we exist exclusively on a diet of red molecular dust bars — you know, *bricks?* — Just like these — the ones that make up Senior Square? And I haven't had a good aged brick in a couple of light years, although mom's homemade pumpernickle bread comes close. She says we've got to eat earth food so that we'll "fit in".

(Touching the edge of the Square)

Look at this mortar — M-mmmmmmmmmmmmmm. The filling's the best part. I always liked to take two bricks, pull 'em apart, scrape the filling off each side with my teeth and then eat the bricks separately. A Kratonian Oreo. Yum! And then ya wash it down with a big, frosty glass of fresh milk. You got milk on Earth, right?

(Bending forward)

These bricks are ready for picking!

(Pulling back)

But I can't chow down on Senior Square — much as I'd like to. Folks would just freak.

(Pause)

(Looking up)

Wow! You can see Venus tonight. Have ya been there? Oh — you really should go. The atmosphere's a little stuffy, but they've got a great rock band there that's out of this world.

(Holding his hands to his temples again)

Okay mom! I'm on my way. Does she have to send out those waves at the very *second* dinner is ready? Hope it's not pot roast again. *(pause)* Wow, I'm starving. Sure could use a quick snack to tide me over.

(Reaching down to the brick wall)

Do you think they'd miss just one?

(Lights out)

* * * *

YOUNG BEAR

A young, native American boy steps forth to Center Stage.

I just don't see how someone named Myrtle Flugelmeyer could get up enough attitude to laugh at *my* name — but she *always* does. *Young Bear.* Is that such a funny name? *(pause)* Well okay, so the last name's Sarducci, but I can't help that. My ole man took the surname of the Bureau of Indian Affairs agent when he left the reservation and the guy's name was Tony Sarducci. See, you can have a real tough time in America when you're last name's Running Fox or Happy Moon. And believe me, a first name like Young Bear causes more than enough problems for ya. *(pause)* People ask me: "Are you Puerto Rican? Are you Mexican? Are you Spanish?" No, I tell 'em. "Then what foreign country are you from?" America, I say, and they freak out. I haven't lied, though, because today, as far as the Indian is concerned, America *is* a foreign country.

(Looking down at and back and forth at Senior Square)

Senior Square! Somethin' else, isn't it? The way it just sits here on land that used to belong to *Native* Americans. *(pause)* Ever think about that? Senior Square is on *Indian* land. That's right. The *whole* country is Indian land. You hang out at the Arcade? Yeah, the Arcade? It's on Indian land. Your room? You go up into your room? Your room, the stairs leadin' up to your room, in fact, your *whole* house *and* the garage is on *Indian* land. Anybody in your family dead? Yeah, that's right. Dead. They buried in this country? Uh. Huh. Then they're up to their *ears* in Indian land. It's the truth. Any history teacher 'ill tell ya that. You wanna get offa Indian land — man — you gotta go to Europe.

(Pause)

Ya know, I'm thinkin' 'bout taking my ole man's last name back. Uh-huh. *(pause)* Oh — it's Red Cliff. No, not Radcliff. *Red Cliff.* Yeah. Young Bear Red Cliff. Sings, don't it? See, I don't want to be white kid, because I'm *not* a white kid. And I'm not ashamed of who I am or where I come from either, so I think I'll go all the way and do the Indian trip to the hilt. *(pauses)* Guys in P.E. call me Tonto. Yeah, they say "Hey Tonto, where's your horse?" Yeah, they give it to me good, sometimes, but I'll tell ya somethin', if they ever *saw* me ride a horse, they'd shut their mouths quick. I broke bucks when I was just a kid of seven, back in Oklahoma.

On the reservation? *Before* we'd changed our last name? And still had some idea of who and what we were? Man, I flew like the wind on the back a Charade. Charade? He was my first horse — a white palomino. He could give some stiff competition to a Harley in a bike against horse race — I'll tell ya that. Oh them old days — hot air in my face, desert dirt flyin' up to the moon as me and Charade cut a path across that Oklahoma desert. Days gone by. Lost days. Back on the plains with the lightin' cracklin' 'cross the sky and the wet, red clay smellin' like the first dawn.

They made a musical about Oklahoma — but I don't remember much singin' and dancin' when I was a kid. Still, we had some good times. Then we came up here to the "civilized" country, so my old man could get work. He's been on unemployment and welfare since the day we arrived. Livin's hard here. Rents are high, our place is small, and the food ain't fresh like it used to be when you shot it yourself. Naw. Back home, I *never* felt like I was livin' on a reservation. But I do now.

Lots a Native Americans have given up — you know, the battle? Took their defeat — like a poison you're forced to swallow. Not me. A warrior in a housing project is still a warrior. *(pause)* Hey! Ya know what I'm gonna do?

(Slapping his leg in an excited fashion)

Wow, I can't believe I just thought of this! Next year? When I'm a senior? Wow, here's what I'm gonna do! I am *riding* into Senior Square. That's right! On the back of a white Palomino. I know. It's tough finding one in the ghetto, but believe or not, I already got one lined up. That's right. I *found* a stable in this neighborhood and it's full of top breed horses. They call it the "Polo Grounds"? Polo! Ain't *that* a sport for rich white men. Man you gotta have millions a dollars just to get a saddle for one 'a them horses. But I know they'll let me borrow one. After all, that Polo stable is on *Indian* land. That's right. They don't wanna make no trouble with *me*.

Yeah, let's see. I'll get Little Cloud — the Apachee kid? And Rock and Roll — the Shawnee twins? Yeah! That's it! Wow! Well *raid* Senior Square! Uh-huh! An authentic Indian raid, right here — in the middle of Central High. We're gonna capture the Square and claim it as Indian land — because it is.

Oh! The prinicpal's gonna freak out, but with his affirmative action policy and all — there's no way he's gonna do anything about it — won't want to tee off the tribal chiefs or the NAANA. NAANA! The National Association for the Advancement of Native Americans. It's a group I started. We only got four members so far, but they're all really dedicated.

I can't wait for the day 'a that raid! They'll be newspapermen and TV people latchin' on to Senior Square like a pile 'a termites on a Totem Pole. And then, when all the cameras are runnin' and everything, I'll calmly walk out of the Square like I'm givin' up. The press 'ill ask me questions, but I won't say nuthin', I'll just keep walkin'. They'll forget about me and go back to the Indians who are still holed up inside this ole brick wigwam and just about when it looks like all the commotion's over — here I'll come — flyin' into the schoolyard on the back of Charade II — a pure bred, white Palomino.

Sure, he'll be a pony not a *real* Palomino horse, but I don't think mosta these people around here 'ill even notice. Reporter's will scatter in all directions and the wh-o-o-osh! — I'll fly over these walls and land smack dab in the middle of Senior Square — right next to that big ole tree there. I'm bound to get on the six o'clock *and* the eleven o'clock news.

Oh, they'll eventually get us out of there and take the territory back — like they always do, but for a moment anyway, we'll be in there — all the Indians in the ghetto — and we'll let the world know that we're still here and we're still fightin'.

(As he starts to walk offstage, he takes a tomahawk out of his back pocket and raises it into the air)

Think it'd be goin' too far to *scalp* Myrtle Flugelmeyer?

(Lights out)

* * * * *

KENNETH EUGENE

The sound of a fist slamming against an open palm. KENNETH EUGENE walks out on stage, punching his hand.

Do you think the Pope was ever a teenager? I have my doubts. Can't imagine him in a pair of cut-off jeans drinking Coke and listening to records. Or surfing. Guess they don't do much of that in Poland anyway. What if he came to Senior Square and blessed the bricks? Wouldn't that be somethin'? The Pope? In Senior Square? Afterwards, you could probably sell each brick for twenty bucks a piece. 'Course, I wouldn't.

This is my second day at Central High and the first time I've gone to public school. Been on the parochial circuit since kindergarten — studying history and math with nuns and priests. Strange comin' to school without a uniform — kids all dressing the way they want. All those bright colored clothes. Distracts me. Especially the girls'. Got through a complete school day without a prayer session yesterday. I know my knees appreciated the break. Whispered a couple 'a Hail Marys on my way to P.E. though. Since my scholarship ran out, my parents had to pull in the ole purse strings and my private Catholic High School was the first luxury to go.

You a Catholic? No?

(Pause. Pointing to the back of the audience)

Oh, yea — there's one! — Way in the back. I can tell by
the guilty look on your face.

(Pause)

Catholicism is a complex religion — lots of accessories —
crosses, scapulars, prayer cards, candles, wafers — ya
gotta go on a shopping spree before you're even ready to
enter the church. It's kind of like the Boy Scouts, ya know?
You need all this gear before you're ready to take the
hike. Catholicism *is* peculiar. But it's been my life. I was
an altar boy, a pre-Seminarian, a volunteer at all the
Parish rummage sales, helped old ladies across the street,
even set my parakeet free — a regular St. Francis Junior.
Of course my parents want me to become a priest but
they were more than grateful that I haven't got hooked
on drugs or joined a rock group.

Sure miss my old school. And even though things are
tight, I'll bet mom and dad could've helped me stay at All
Saints High. They bought me and my brother Mark
Charles — we all have *two* first names — a word pro-
cessor last month. Said it would help us do our homework quicker. That thing could 'av paid for my junior year.

(Pause)

Yeah. So if my parents won't let to me go to Catholic
School anymore, well, maybe I just might not *be* a

Catholic anymore. Maybe I'll be Jewish! My friend Arnie is Jewish and they seem to have it made. I mean, it's a *fun* religion. More holidays, better food, and they're havin' a party for somebody or somethin' every time you turn around.

And — even if your parents are only middle class, you still stand an excellent chance of nailing a free summer trip to Isreal by the time you graduate from high school. Wait! There's more! On your thirteenth birthday, they throw this huge party for ya, right? All your relatives come and they each give you money! That's what I call religion. I wonder if it's too late for *me* to have a Bar Mitzvah?

(Pause)

Know what a Catholic kid gets on his thirteenth birthday? A cake. I know! A lousy cake. How can that compete with cash? I can sure go for a faith that throws a lot of bucks into a kid's direction. Those extra bucks help to keep your belief in your fellow man.

And Jews go to church on Saturday. I like that. Get it out of the way quick — take the rest of the weekend off. 'Course, I wouldn't get to hang out with all my friends at the Arcade on Saturday — but then, on the other hand, I'd get to sleep *late* on Sunday. Yeah, I could work it out. And I like the Jewish sins better, too. In Judaism, if you do something bad — it's a sin, but in Catholicism, if you just *think* about doing something bad, you've committed a sin. And if you think about *thinking* about a sin, it's a sin, so you're in trouble from the word go. I mean, by the time you realize you're having a bad thought, it's too late, you've had it.

I'm gonna check out some other religions, too. I mean, I'm for eternal life, ya know? So I'll always be lookin' for the best road to heaven.

(Pause)

I wonder how dad'd like it if I became a Mormon? They believe in double and *triple* marriages, a great idea — but Donny and Marie are Mormons, hmmm, don't think I could handle *that.* Maybe Buddhism? Oh, but I'd look really bad without hair. How 'bout the Trappist Monks? 'Course they have to get up every morning at the crack 'o dawn and make all that jelly. Could join the Protestants. — What do they do anyway? They don't make jelly, shave their heads, or give out leaflets. So, whadda they do? The Jehovah's Witnesses! Naw — that leaflet thing reminds me too much of my days as a paper boy. So many religions! Talk about confusing! I wonder if God has as much trouble figuring out what church to go to as I do? And I wonder if He takes attendance to see who goes and who doesn't? He couldn't be as strict about the attendance thing as Miss Melbourne, though.

There's alotta religions to pick 'n choose from, that's for sure. But with all things said and done — this Jewish thing looks *pre-tty* good to me. Let's see —

(Adding on his fingers)

The Jews give ya — money on your birthday, *and* that big party, a trip to Israel — Sundays off. And the Catholics give ya — a *cake* on your birthday! That's it! Well, seems clear to me. Maybe I'll change my name from Kenneth Eugene Williams to Kenneth David Williamsberg. Yeah. I like it. I know it'll make my mother cry. But I like it.

(Looking to the Square)

Saint Ann's, Saint Luke's, Saint Joseph's, Saint Michael's — all the ground work I've done to prepare for that big final exam in the sky and I wind up here in Saint Senior Square. In a way, it's *kind* of like a holy place, I guess — not like the wailing wall or Vatican Square. But people hang out here and they kind of check out what's happening with their lives, you know; they stop for a couplea seconds and think about where they're goin' and maybe help each other out now 'n then. And I call a place that does somethin' like that to ya, *pre*-tty close to holy. And I'd call people who hang out in a place like that *almost* religious — in their own way, a' course. Though I doubt they'll ever make Wookie Pennsicola into an altar boy.

Next year *I'll* be in Senior Square — maybe just another Catholic kid looking for some answers, or *maybe* as a Jewish boy, with a mother in therapy.

(He walks off stage singing "Hava Nagaila")

(Fade out)

* * * * *

BETTY JEAN

A slight, underweight young girl, with a ponytail, wearing jeans and a thin, peach-colored blouse, timidly walks on stage.

It's really best that I can't go into Senior Square until next year. I might be tempted to sleep there because, right now, well, I have no place to live. *(Pause)* You see, I'm a runaway. I'm sure my parents have the police out looking for me; that's why I'm wearing this disguise. I'm supposed to be a Hare Krishna, but I couldn't find any orange chiffon curtains to wear, so I just slipped on my mother's best peach blouse, put my hair up in a pony tail and prayed I could fake 'em out.

(She pulls out a pipe cleaner and holds it toward the audience like a stick of incense)

Can you say Hare Krishna? Come on. *(Pause)* Huh? I *know* it's a pipe cleaner. How am I supposed to get Pachoulli incense in *my* neighborhood? Can't you just pretend?

(Putting incense away)

I could tell you were the kind of people that wouldn't say Hare Krishna.

(Looking at her watch)

Wow! I've been a runaway for *nine* hours now! Life on the streets is hell! Everything's closed. Can't go shopping. The last picture at the movie house just started running; already missed the beginning.

(Looking up and screaming)

What was *that?* Did you see that thing fly by? What was it? *(pause)* Oh, the horrors a kid on the street sees! Things that would freak out most adults. *(pause)* Bet I'll find my picture on a milk carton in the morning. My mother works fast when she's freaked out. I'm everything to her. She'll go crazy when it really sinks in that I'm gone. She'll cry and say "Betty Jean, I loved her so — she was my life!"

But it'll be too late, because I'll be in Nepal by then. Yep! That's where I'm goin' — Katmandu. Learned all about it on a National Geographic special on TV a couple of weeks ago. You can get married when you're twelve years old in Nepal if ya want to. Ya don't need an ID to drink either, *and* school's over entirely at the age of fifteen! 'Course people only live till about the age 'a forty there, they cut your hands off for shop lifting and there's a hundred different kinds 'a poison insects — but there's no curfew. Yeah, *Katmandu.* They'll never look for me there, because the chance of *my* mother going to any country that doesn't take American Express is nada.

God they abused me! I just couldn't take it anymore. Imagine — taking the VCR out of my bedroom for the whole weekend just because I watched a bootlegged copy of *The Texas Chainsaw Massacre Murder* after my mother refused to have it in the house. Give me a break, I'm almost fourteen years old. I'm confused. I'm angry. I *need* to see innocent people butchered with a chainsaw from time to time, okay? It's a release. Just like walking into Senior Square. *(pause)* Should I? Should I go into Senior Square even though I'm just a freshman? I can see the headlines now "Tortured Teen Escapes from Suburban Nightmare — Trespassing Tenth Grader Confesses to Senior Square Invasion." I don't know — I'm *still* on detention for crashing the Senior Pizza Party last week. Snuck into Senior Hall with an empty pizza box and posed as a delivery girl. *Two weeks* after school — for hoisting a lousy slice of soggy, senior pizza.

(Looking offstage and shouting)

Hi Ramona! Can you lend me five dollars? *(pause)* Because I'm homeless, that's why! *(pause)* Being on the streets has taken away all my dignity and now I've been reduced to begging for money from home room monitors like Ramona Saratoga.

(Shouting)

Ramona please! *(Pause)* Her father's worth millions but she won't even kick in a fin to help an abused teen with no place to sleep. If I had a fake ID, I could sell my blood and make forty dollars, then I could get a motel room, but I don't so I can't.

I'll bet my mom's refilled her valium prescription by now. She's probably figured out I'm never coming back. Mother's have a special sixth sense that tells him when they've failed their children and lost them forever. Ten years will pass, but she'll never forget this day. It will haunt her for the rest of her life. *(pause)* Got a cigarette? Yes, I know it isn't *ladylike* to smoke, but now that I'm on the streets, I've got to pick up a few disgusting habits so that I'll blend in. Maybe I'll put on a pair of panty hose and then roll them down around my ankles. That's pretty disgusting isn't it? Then, I'll shave *one* leg, but not the other. Really? That's going too far, huh? God! I'm so *immature!* But I wear it well — don't you think?

Can't wait for the eleven o'clock news tonight. I'll probably have to throw on a layer of cheap red lipstick and sneak into a bar to watch it. I know it'll be worth it, though. I can just see it now.

(She does an impression of the news)

I'm Chuck Chuckley and *this* is the eleven o'clock news. Police are continuing their search tonight for missing teenager Betty Jean Kay. An all points bulletin has been issued around the world in the hopes of finding the runaway daughter of Mr. and Mrs. E.G. Kay of Maplewood Drive. Then they'll run a video of my mother crying frantically as my dad holds her up. Mrs. Kay was *hysterical* when she realized that she had totally failed as a parent and therefore caused her highly intelligent, attractive daughter Betty Jean to take to the streets. Police are combing the talent agencies, video parlors and saloons this evening in the hopes of finding the pretty young girl. Several modeling agencies who saw Betty Jean's picture in the evening paper tonight are prepared at this time to offer her lucrative contracts and two television producers have already called the studio to inquire as to the possibility of Miss Kay appearing in a guest spot on Miami Vice. Once again, Betty Jean Kay has vanished.

I hope I won't be *totally* wiped out by the time I get to Senior Square. By then, I'll have been on the streets for three years. I'll be tough and unlikely to trust most people, especially friendly strangers offering me rides in their Lincoln Continentals. How can I stay in school by day and sleep in dumpsters by night? Maybe I'll write a book about my experiences and when it becomes a best seller, I'll lease the rights to the networks for a TV movie and then I can use that money to buy my own condo and beauty parlor.

(Looking at her watch)

Nine hours and twenty-three minutes on the streets. The life cycle of many insects is only ten to twelve hours. I've been out here for nearly an entire generation.

(Going through her pockets for change)

I've got to call my mother! I know, I know it's a dumb move. I'll make it quick because she'll probably have the call traced and in a couple of minutes, the police will be swarming all over Senior Square like a bunch of junior-highers who've never read the student handbook. I'm gonna have to drop the receiver and run as soon as I make the call, if I want to have any chance at all of getting away, but I've *got* to call her. I'm sure she's on the verge of suicide by now, and I don't want that on my conscience.

(Puts money in a payphone next to Senior Square)

I'm just gonna let her know that I'm all right and then, I'm dropping the phone.

(She dials)

Hello — maw? It's me,

(She makes scratchy noises to fake a bad connection)

Yeah maw, it's me — Betty Jean. Sorry we've got such a bad connection but the phone service is terrible here in *The Carribean.* Huh? *(pause)* What? No, I'm *not* calling you from upstairs in my room. I'm not *in* my room. I'm not in the house. I'm not even in *the* country! I know you're not in the mood for jokes; this isn't a joke. I ran away, maw, I'm on the streets! Didn't you get my note? My note! My *runaway note!* I wrote it on the side of a Bloomingdale's shopping bag and left it on the kitchen table. *(pause)* You threw the bag out! Without reading my note! I know you've very busy — but you got a runaway daughter here; can't you take five seconds from your nail polishing and read the note that's going to change your life forever? *(pause)* Yes, I *know* dinner's almost ready and *no I'm not*

coming home, not after the way you treated me over that
Texas Chainsaw Massacre Murder thing. What are you
having for dinner? Fried chicken? Mashed potatoes?
And the gravy made from the little crunchy things that
you fried the chicken in? Well, you can eat it by yourself
tonight because I'll be in Bimini before you even get to
dessert. Bimini. *Bimini!* It's an island in the Carribean. A
strawberry pie? With whipped cream? The Carribean!
It's an ocean? *And* an apple pie, too?

(Covering the mouthpiece)

She's a complete wreck! She only cooks like that when
he's on the verge of suicide.

(Back to the phone)

What do you mean if I don't come home you're inviting
the Montgomerys over? Edith Montgomery eats like a
starving dog; there won't be a crumb left!

(Covering the mouthpiece)

She's going to take every sleeping pill in the house if I
don't get over there.

(Back to the phone)

All right. All right, mom. I'll take the next water shuttle
out of St. Thomas. Yes. Yes. I should be home in about—

(She looks at her watch)

Fifteen minutes. Huh? A loaf of rye bread? The Store 24?
Okay. Right. Okay. See you soon.

(She hangs up)

I've just saved the life of a highly *materialistic* middle aged
housewife. Someday, she'll thank me. It's gonna take her
months to get over this. But in the long run, I think it'll
turn out to be a good thing. It'll help her to realize how
important I am in her life and maybe she'll think twice
before touching my VCR again. I'll go back. For now. I
suppose I owe her that.

(As she exits)

And besides, it's really tough to get good chicken gravy
on the streets.

* * * * *

CANDY

A young woman in a wheelchair rolls onto the stage.

I don't see why they're makin' me go to another school. Do you? I passed all the exams for the year and graduated into the twelfth grade yesterday. So, they let me become a senior early because next year I'll be going to a special school that's "accessible." Central High's *accessible* enough for me. Sure, there's alotta little hills — and no ramps leadin' into the classrooms, but I get by. Candy Johansen is a survivor! Why does everybody make such a big deal about my being handicapped? People get so upset because I've lost the use of my legs. So what? What do I need legs for?

(Grabbing the wheels of the chair and spinning around)

I've got wheels! Who wants to run when you can ro-o-o-o-ll!

There are a few things that do bug me, though. Like sailin' into the ladies' room, opening the door to the handicapped stall and finding a bunch of freshmen girls hiding in there and smoking cigarettes. Life in the cafeteria is a pain, too. Like I'm waiting in line to get my lunch? And all the kids standin' around me are holdin' their trays over my head and eating half their food while the crumbs

77

are fallin' off the plates like a hail storm and landing on the top of my head?

(Brushing crumbs off her head and shoulders)

Makes me feel like a dust pan on wheels.

And what *really* blows my cool is when I'm rockin' down the sidewalk and I get to the edge of the curb? And five people rush up to me and say: "Be careful! Can I help you?" I mean, I travel up and down the hills leading to Central High, side swipe the potholes on Main Street and plod up those three fat steps leading to my front porch, but I can't roll off a four-inch curb without the aid of the entire neighborhood? Sometimes I wanna turn to these people and say—

(Loudly) This is a *curb* not the Grand Canyon! But I 'spoze they're just tryin' to be nice — like the other day, I was just about to cross Main Street? And this boy scout guy rushes out from nowhere and says "Let me help you!" He gives my chair a huge shove, pushes me too hard — and wham! I go sailing into traffic.

(Grabbing the wheels)

Powerful ball bearings in these babies. I was almost run over! Helpful people can be *very* dangerous.

Today is my first day as a senior, but I never went into that square. Should have. Would of had no problem getting a seat.

(Nervous laugh)

I don't know why I didn't go in there. I just couldn't
do it.

Guess the accident zilched my thirst for adventure. Like I
no longer want to climb Mount Everest, ya know. Is there
a *ramp* on that thing? And here's somethin' funny. I
never liked dancing ya know? Thought it was real stupid,
but now that I'm stuck in this thing, I sure do alotta thinkin' 'bout it. That's the way the brain works — pro-
grammed to want what it can't have. To dream. And you
see, my dream has always been to arrive early in the
morning on my first day in the twelfth grade and walk
proudly into Senior Square, You know — stand tall in the
center of the Square and just look over the walls like I'm
in some castle courtyard or somethin'. Leave my footprints on that senior ground! 'Course, that'll never hap-
pen now. I wanted that first day to be a special one
because my brother, Daryl, dropped out in the ninth
grade and my sister, Judy, got married and dropped out
in the tenth. So I'm the first in my family to just about
make it through high school. After the accident, my folks
didn't think that graduating from high school was that
important. But it was important to me. I was really gonna
plan for that first day as a senior, but life sure does take
care of your pipe dreams for ya. Today especially, I know
why they call this—

(Touching the wheels of her chair)

"physically challenged."

(Looking up and then touching her face)

Did you feel a drop 'a rain?

(Pause)

It's been a challenge, too. Since the accident, I've over-
come a lot of difficulties — first day in school in this
thing, explaining to my teacher why I had to quit P.E.
class, watching my boyfriend say goodbye because he
"Just couldn't deal with it." — I've done some very pain-
ful, necessary things, but I just can't get up the guts to go
into Senior Square. It's like going in there in a wheelchair
would somehow be the final proof that my dream will
never come true. As long as I stay outside, there's a chance,
maybe, that I'll get better and one day I can *walk* into
the square.

(Pause. Holding out her hand)

Yep. That *was* a raindrop. It's dark and I'd better get
home. Senior Square looks like an illusion right now,
doesn't it? — With that flood light shinin' on the picnic
tables and nobody but me around. I wish you could go in
there for a minute and take a look at it from the inside — I
heard that's the best view.

(Pause)

I suppose, I could go in for ya and tell you what it's like. I mean I should go in, I'm a senior now — one of the lucky kids who made it. Maybe I can't make footprints in there—

(Touching the wheels of her chair)

But I can sure make tracks! The square belongs to me, too, and I have a right — *(Pause)* No,

(Looking at her wheelchair)

—not like this. I gotta leave, those clouds are gonna rip open any second. Gotta get home. Got things to do. Important, *things.*

(Rolling to the side of the stage, stopping and then coming back slowly)

No. *(Pause)* It's too late. I can't go.

(Enter ROCHELLE)

   Rochelle. Please go. For *me.* I want to be a senior so bad, but it's one part that I'm still too young to play.

(Enter RAYMO)

   Raymo. Go for me. There's a good chance it'll be twelve years before *I* become a senior.

(Enter SUZANNE)

Suzanne. Go for me and my baby and Nicky. Show me I still have a chance to make it.

(Enter PAT)

Pat. Go for me. And for all the future women presidents of Senior Square. And all the future women presidents of the world. And all the future women presidents of the universe. And all the fut—

(Enter the RAPPER, pushing PAT out of the way)

Rapper.
Go for me into that Senior Square,
Until I do my time,
You can sit in there.
Show *me* what it's like to be free,
Go for me, go for me, for me.

(Enter NATHAN)

Nathan. Go for me. I need to be part of something courageous in my life.

(Enter JACK)

Jack. Go for me. I need someone to show the way.

(Enter ARBADELLA. She attempts to step forth in the square)

ARBADELLA. I can go for myself, girl! *(She steps forward and is stopped by the other players)* Course, on th' other hand, Miss Johnson might be watchin' from a bush.

(Enter NUMBER 12)

NUMBER 12. Go for me. It's as close to outer space as you're ever gonna get.

(Enter YOUNG BEAR)

YOUNG BEAR. Go for me and my people and all the people who will never have a chance to go.

(Enter KENNETH EUGENE)

KENNETH EUGENE. Go for me. And all the Catholics and all the Jews. Yeah! Go for *me!*

(Enter BETTY JEAN)

BETTY JEAN. Go for me. And my mother. On second thought — could you take my mother with you?

ALL IN UNISON. *(Except CANDY)* Go for us — show the way.

(The cast moves close to CANDY and touches the back of her chair. Long pause while CANDY decides)

CANDY. Well, I guess there's no point in letting my *whole* dream die— *(A slow drumbeat begins)* I can still save part of it — I can still take my place on the *edge* of my dream.

(Dramatic music arises in the background as the drumbeat grows louder. Then the thunder and lightning begins. She rolls to stage center, then back a little)

CANDY. Spike Paletti — you're not the only one who can score a touchdown! *(Pause. She rolls forward very slowly, hesitates, then stops)*

(The students standing behind her applaud and cheer as they chant:)

STUDENTS. *(In unison, loudly)*
GO! GO! GO!

They reach out to the audience and try to get them to participate in the chanting)

STUDENTS. GO! GO! GO! GO! GO! GO!

(Softer)

Go. Go. Go.

(Even softer)

Go. Go. Go.

(VERY soft, fading to a whisper)

Go. Go. Go. Go. Go. Go.

(Suddenly, CAST is silent. Pause)

CANDY. *Nobody.* Steals. My. Dream!

(CANDY grabs the wheels and gives herself one big shove.)

Lights Out.

THE END

PROPS

ESSENTIAL
Large book (for dictionary)

Leaflets (Can be mock, but if distributed to the audience they should read): "Ban High School Now — Stop the Oppression of the Teenage Masses" — Pat Johnson for Senior President.

A pipe cleaner

Can of spray paint

Basketball

"Ghetto box" (huge radio with tape recorder.) Can be mock with sound coming from recorder offstage.

Wheelchair (manual *not* electric)

Hatchet (Tomahawk)

Tourniquet, hypodermic needle (can be made)
Spoon, matches

OPTIONAL
Rochelle's make-up (pancake, powder, eye make-up, lipstick, rouge)

SOUND

Drums. Necessary for the finale. Can be prerecorded but to assure a coordinated beat that coincides with Candy's speech, live drums are recommended.

Dramatic music. This can be anything "dramatic" that the producer chooses. Instrumental of Love Theme from "An Officer and a Gentleman" ("Lift Us Up Where We Belong,") by Buffy Sante-Marie, is one suggestion, but any instrumental that clearly conveys tension will suffice.

PRODUCTION NOTES

Since each monologue in the play is a complete dramatic piece, it is possible to drop one or two of them where casting or time is a problem. Role doubling is also possible.

You are also encouraged to substitute Central High with the name of your own school. Teacher's names in the play may also be substituted with the names of your own teachers, where applicable, and if desired.